V for what?

My Kid Words Series (Book V)

Learn 30 Words Starting with Letter V and Learn Little Information about those Words.

V for Vase

A vase is a jar, usually made of glass or pottery, used for holding cut flowers or as an ornament.

V for Vacuum cleaner

A vacuum cleaner is a device that cleans dust and dirt from floors. Sometimes it is just called a vacuum because it uses the force of a vacuum to suck dirt into a large chamber from which it can be dumped into the garbage.

V for Valise

A valise is a small suitcase. If you're carrying a valise as you climb onto a train, you're probably heading off on a short vacation or a weekend trip.

V for Valve

A device that regulates the flow of a fluid in a pipe or other enclosure is called a valve. Valves control flow by means of a movable part that opens to allow the fluid to flow, closes to block the fluid, or partially obstructs an opening in a passageway to slow the fluid's flow.

V for Vane

A vane or wind vane is an instrument that can measure wind direction. Wind is moving air, and it pushes on the tail of the wind vane, causing it to turn so that the arrow points in the direction from which the wind is blowing.

V for Vault

A vault is a secure room where money and other valuable things can be kept safely. Most of the money was in storage in bank vaults.

V for Ventilation system

A ventilation system is a structure that controls airflow inside buildings. Its main function is to constantly supply fresh air, usually from the outside, while sending stale air back out.

V for Vaccine

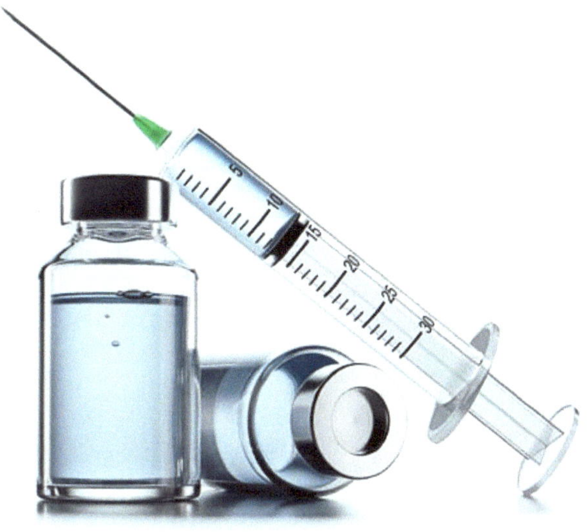

Vaccines are substances that prevent the spread of disease. Giving people vaccines can save millions of lives. For example, smallpox killed some 2 million people in 1967. By 1979 the disease had disappeared. This change resulted from a worldwide program of vaccination.

V for Vial

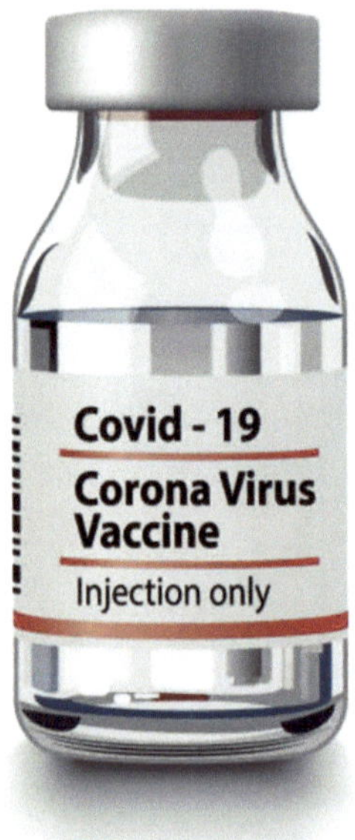

Vial is a small container (as for medicines) made usually of glass or plastic.

V for Vessel

Each one is a type of vessel. A vessel can be a ship or large boat, or a tube that transports blood throughout your body.

V for Van

A van is a small or medium-sized road vehicle with one row of seats at the front and a space for carrying goods behind.

V for Video

Video is an electronic medium for the recording, copying, playback, broadcasting, and display of moving visual media. The first video to be uploaded to YouTube is entitled "Me at the Zoo". YouTube's co-founder Jawed Karim uploaded the 18-second clip on 23rd April 2005.

V for Vest

A vest is an undergarment worn on the upper part of the body. There are different types of vests. Some vests use fashion, and others vests use them for a different kind of safety.

V for Visor

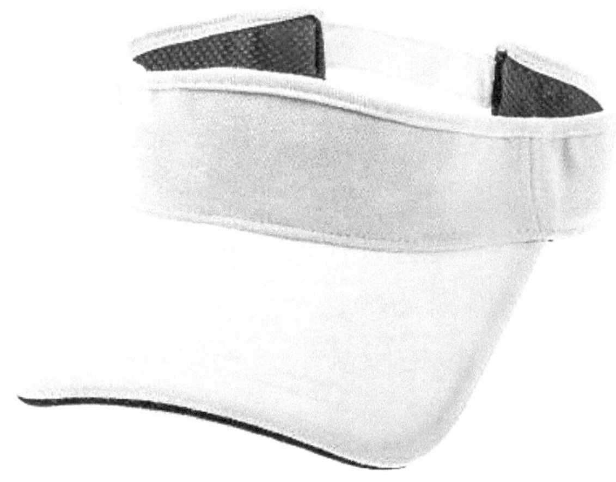

A visor is a surface that protects the eyes, such as shading them from the sun or other bright light or protecting them from objects.

V for Vampire

Vampires are fictional blood sucking night creatures. They are immortal and are said to mostly survive on human blood. They have fangs and usually bite the neck of humans and suck blood from it. They can also drink from the vein in the thigh.

V for Vampire bat

Vampire bats glide stealthily through the night air as they search for food. Like the legendary monster that they're named after, these small mammals drink the blood of other animals for survival. They feed on cows, pigs, horses, and birds.

V for Vine Snake

Vine snakes are often also known as Asian vine snakes. This name is due to the fact that the Asian vine snake is one of the most common snakes found in Asia.

V for Viper

The vipers are a group of poisonous snakes that have sharp fangs. There are about 200 species, or types, of viper. They are found throughout the world except in Australia and Antarctica.

V for Viperfish

A viperfish is any species of marine fish in the genus Chauliodus. Viperfish are characterized by long, needle-like teeth and hinged lower jaws. A typical viperfish grows to lengths of 30 to 60 cm (12 to 23.5 in). The viperfish uses this light organ to attract its prey through a process known as bioluminescence. By flashing the light on and off, it can be used like a fishing lure to attract smaller fish.

V for Vegetable

Vegetables are the leaves, stems, roots, or other parts of certain plants that people eat. Vegetables usually come from herbaceous plants. Herbaceous plants have stems that are softer than the woody stems of bushes and trees.

V for Vanilla

Vanilla comes from beans that grow on certain types of orchids in warm parts of the world. Madagascar, Indonesia, and China produce large amounts of vanilla. A vanilla orchid has a long climbing stem that attaches itself to a tree trunk or pole. Vanilla beans are the fruit of the plant.

V for Vanilla ice cream

Vanilla ice cream is the most common and basic flavor of ice cream which is favorite amongst all. Vanilla ice cream is made by blending in vanilla essence in along with the eggs (optional), cream, milk and sugar. The vanilla essence added gives the ice cream a very natural aroma and vanilla flavor.

V for Vinegar

Vinegar is a sour liquid that is used to flavor and preserve food. It is made by putting alcohol through a chemical change called fermentation. The word vinegar comes from the French words for sour wine. Vinegar that is made from grapes is called wine vinegar. But vinegar can be made from other foods as well.

V for Vitamins

Vitamins are nutrient that the body needs in small amounts to function and stay healthy. Sources of vitamins are plant and animal food products and dietary supplements. Some vitamins are made in the human body from food products.

V for Veins

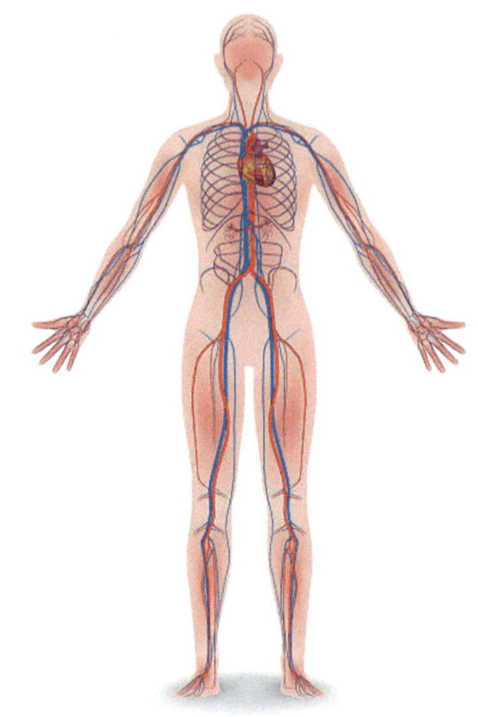

A vein is a type of blood vessel in the body. All veins carry blood to the heart. Most veins carry blood that is low in oxygen, except for the pulmonary vein and the umbilical veins which carry blood that is high in oxygen.

V for Vomit

It goes by many names: vomit, throw up, upchuck, gut soup, ralphing, and barf. Whatever you call it, it's the same stuff: mushed-up, half-digested food or liquid that gets mixed with spit and stomach juices as it makes a quick exit up your throat and out of your mouth.

V for Violin

Violin is a stringed musical instrument with four strings that is usually held against the shoulder under the chin and played with a bow.

V for Volleyball

Volleyball is a team sport in which players use their hands or arms to knock a ball over a net. Two teams, usually with six players each, compete in a volleyball game. Volleyball can be played inside, in a gym, or outside, on a beach or in a park.

V for Volcano

A volcano is a mountain or hill with an opening. When a volcano erupts, magma is pushed up through the opening with great force. When magma reaches the Earth's surface, it is called lava. Lava can be as hot as 2,200°F (1,204°C).

V for Venus

Venus is the second planet from the Sun and is Earth's closest neighbor in the solar system. Venus is the brightest object in the sky after the Sun and the Moon, and sometimes looks like a bright star in the morning or evening sky. The planet is a little smaller than Earth and is similar to Earth inside.

Check out other books in this series·

www.ingramcontent.com/pod-product-compliance
Lightning Source LLC
Chambersburg PA
CBHW040949110726
48006CB00007B/1317